ATOMS, NATURE, AND MAN

ATOMS, NATURE, AND MAN

NEAL O. HINES

ISBN: 978-93-90215-13-3

Published: -

LECTOR HOUSE LLP
E-MAIL: lectorpublishing@gmail.com

THE UNDERSTANDING THE ATOM SERIES

Nuclear energy is playing a vital role in the life of every man, woman, and child in the United States today. In the years ahead it will affect increasingly all the peoples of the earth. It is essential that all Americans gain an understanding of this vital force if they are to discharge thoughtfully their responsibilities as citizens and if they are to realize fully the myriad benefits that nuclear energy offers them.

The United States Atomic Energy Commission provides this booklet to help you achieve such understanding.

Edward J. Brunenkant, Director Division of Technical Information

UNITED STATES ATOMIC ENERGY COMMISSION

Dr. Glenn T. Seaborg, Chairman
James T. Ramey
Wilfrid E. Johnson
Dr. Theos J. Thompson
Dr. Clarence E. Larson

ATOMS, NATURE, AND MAN

MAN-MADE RADIOACTIVITY IN THE ENVIRONMENT

BY

NEAL O. HINES

THE COVER

Scientists aboard a seagoing vessel prepare to study contents of a plankton net as part of their research into radioactivity in an oceanic environment.

THE AUTHOR NEAL O. HINES

Is an established writer and experienced academic administrator with an unusual background in radiobiological surveys of the Pacific Ocean atomic test sites. He holds degrees from Indiana and Northwestern Universities. A former journalism teacher at the University of California and Assistant to the President of the University of Washington, Mr. Hines also worked for a number of years with the Laboratory of Radiation Biology of the University of Washington, where he served from 1961-1963 as administrative assistant and as Executive Secretary of the Advisory Council on Nuclear Energy and Radiation for the State of Washington. He was a member of the survey teams visiting Bikini and Eniwetok in 1949 and 1956 and Christmas Island in 1962. His "Bikini Report" (*Scientific Monthly*, February 1951) was one of the earliest descriptions of radiobiological studies in the Pacific. He is the author of *Proving Ground* (University of Washington Press, 1962), a detailed history of radiobiological studies in the Pacific from 1946-1961.

CONTENTS

INTRODUCTION

Mankind, increasingly crowding the earth, modifies the earthly environment in uncounted subtle and unpredictable ways, too rarely to the benefit of either earth or man. In this century it has become critically important that we comprehend more precisely than ever before the biological mechanisms and balances of our environment and that we learn to detect changes and to understand what they imply.

The release of atomic energy added a new dimension to the possibility of environmental change. In man's first experiments with atomic energy, he added small but perceptible amounts of radioactivity to the earth's natural total; as the Atomic Age matures, he inevitably will add more. But, in the course of his experiments, man has come to realize that environmental and biological studies, which now are necessary because of the use of atomic energy, may help solve not only the problems atomic energy creates but also the larger problem of how to manage wisely the world's limited natural resources.

This booklet describes the environmental investigations that have been conducted with the aid of the atom since the first atomic detonation near Alamogordo, New Mexico, in 1945. The earth's mysteries, however, are not easily unlocked, and investigations of our environment with atomic tools have only begun. The story thus is one of beginnings—but of beginnings that point the way, it is hoped, to a new understanding of the world in the atomic future.

SOME PRELIMINARY IDEAS

Biologists are interested in every kind of living thing. When they study organisms in relation to atomic radiations, they enter the field of radiobiology, which really is not a science in itself but merely a branch of the larger interest in biology. Biologists find that atomic energy has significance both in the study of individual organisms and in studies of organisms in their natural communities and habitats.

Skin-diving biologist collecting giant clam from coral bottom of Bikini Lagoon in the Pacific Ocean.

Radioactivity introduced into any community may be "taken up" by the biological system, becoming subject to cycling in food chains or to accumulation in plant or animal tissues. The presence of radioactivity permits study of the workings of a system as large as an ocean, perhaps, or of one no larger than a tree. And in each case it thus may be possible to observe how the cycles of organic renewal are related to the larger systems of life on earth.

THE SINGLE ENVIRONMENT

The environment in which we live is recognizable as a single complex, composed of many subenvironments—land, oceans, atmosphere, and the space beyond our envelope of air. The deer in the forest, the lizard in the desert burrow, and the peavine in the meadow are different kinds of organisms living in situations that are seemingly unalike. Each creature is part of its environment and a contributor to it, but it also is part of the total biosphere.[1] All creatures are linked to each other, however remotely, in their dependence on limited environments that together form the whole of nature.

Gray shark photographed in another Pacific lagoon.

We know much about the life of the earth, but there is far more that we do not know. Understanding of the large cyclical forces has continued to elude us. We do not even yet grasp the small and seemingly random biological relations between individual organisms—relations involving predator and prey, for instance, and those among species and families—such as exist together in symbiotic[2] harmony and interdependence. Through centuries of observation we have gained a store of information. We are left, however, with a still unsatisfied curiosity about the reach and strength of the tenuous biological cords that bind together the lives of the deer, the lizard, and the peavine.

THE NEED TO UNDERSTAND

Life on earth evolved amid constant exposure to ionizing[3] radiation, from

[1] The biosphere is the living world, the sum of all living, interacting organisms.

[2] Symbiosis is a condition in which two organisms or communities of organisms live together in close association, either on a basis of mutual benefit or of benefit to one only, with or without harm to the other.

[3] Ionizing radiation is radiation that can cause damage to biological tissues.

the earth itself and from space, known as background radiation. Therefore environmental studies must be conducted in relation to, and with understanding of, background radioactivity.

This Pacific Ocean coconut crab, member of a family that usually sticks to tide-covered beaches, depends on coconut trees for its food.

Of some 340 kinds of atoms that have been found in nature, about 70 are radioactive. Three families of radioactive isotopes[4]—the uranium, thorium, and actinium series—produce a large proportion of the natural radiation. Other radionuclides[5] occur singly, rather than in families, and some of them, such as potassium-40 and carbon-14, are major contributors of natural radioactivity. Traces of natural radioactivity can be found, in fact, in all substances on earth.

When man began experimenting with atomic fusion and fission, he placed in his environment—across vast landscapes, in the oceans, and in the atmosphere—measurable additional amounts of radioactivity. These additions were composed of the longer-lived members of some 200 kinds of atomic radiation. Although the additions constituted but a fraction of the background burden, they represented the first alteration of the radiological balance that had existed since the early ages of the planet. Thus it became necessary to determine what the impact of such a change might be. In the process of inquiry, these ideas emerged:

1. The addition of man-made radioactivity presents the possibility of delayed or cumulative effects. Long-term studies, geared to the assessment of biological effects from extremely low radioactivity, are essential.

2. The addition of radioactivity makes possible broad-gauged studies to trace the movement and concentration of radionuclides in the environment. These stud-

[4] Isotopes are variant forms of atoms of the same element.

[5] Nuclides is a term used to describe all the forms of all the atoms. Radionuclides are radioactive nuclides.

ies, in turn, can disclose new information on biological complexes and mechanisms.

A flying atmospheric physics laboratory studying concentration of radionuclides over an Atomic Energy Commission laboratory. Instrument pod under wing samples air to provide a visual record of radioactivity.

Transferring a sample of water taken from the depths of the Columbia River for radiochemical analysis in a laboratory.

The quantities of low-level long-lived radioactivity already released into our environment will provide materials for future studies covering decades. Further, because radioisotopes are chemically similar to nonradioactive forms, observation of their biological fate will provide clues to the transport, concentration, dilution, or elimination of many other kinds of man-made toxic agents and contaminants of the environment.

OPERATING CONCEPTS

Oceanographers bringing aboard a 50-gallon seawater sampler from the ocean depths find it a difficult task, even in moderate seas. This photo was taken aboard the R. V. Crawford in the Atlantic.

Environmental problems are best approached in the environment itself, where all the natural variables and unknowns are present. Laboratory work is essential, but no laboratory can carve from nature or reproduce artificially all the complexities of the natural environmental "laboratory", the ecosystem.[6]

---

[6] An ecosystem is a natural community, taken as a whole, including all biological and

Environmental studies frequently demand the coordinated attentions of ecologists,[7] chemists, physicists, geologists, oceanographers, meteorologists, botanists, zoologists, and others, all working together to approach the environment as a synchronized mechanism.

Finally, environmental studies are conducted with a special consciousness of the need to withhold judgment as to what is meant by "effect", particularly "radiation effect". Gross, immediate effects may be determinable. Ultimate effects may be generations in the making, remote in time and space from their causes. Studies thus are focused on biological processes and on isolation and identification of the long-range trends.

---

environmental factors.

[7] Ecologists are scientists concerned with the interrelations of organisms and their environments.

A VIEW IN PERSPECTIVE, 1946-1963

Bikini Atoll, in the Marshall Islands, represents, in miniature, a world that has experienced all the forces, immediate and residual, that can result from nuclear detonation.

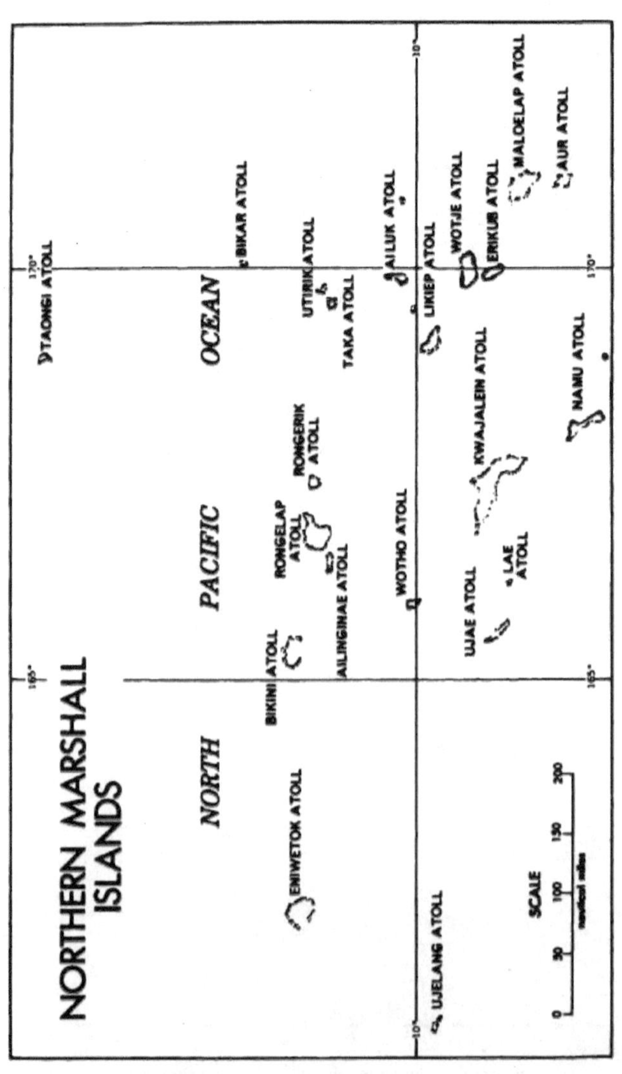

Bikini in 1946 was the scene of the first peacetime tests of atomic weapons. One of these tests involved the detonation of an atomic device under water, in the heart of the atoll's aquatic circulatory system. Bikini also was used for 5 years, from 1954 through 1958, for the testing of thermonuclear[8] devices. Its islands and reefs were burned by atomic heat, and the waters of its lagoon were contaminated by deposits of radioactive fallout. Thus, for almost a score of years, Bikini, a small outcropping of coral in the mid-Pacific, was identified with the earliest experiments in nuclear explosion.

Through the years of testing and later, Bikini also was the site of repeated biological investigations. Teams of scientists examined Bikini annually from 1946 to 1950 and from 1954 to 1958. Then in 1964, after an interlude of 6 years in which Bikini was undisturbed either by weapons tests or human visitors, scientists went there again to make a comprehensive ecological resurvey.

The scientists found in the Bikini ecosystem, in low but perceptible amounts, residual traces of radioactivity deposited by the tests. On certain islands, craters dug by nuclear explosions still gaped in the reefs. The test islands still bore nuclear scars, and in some areas of the lagoon corals and algae had been killed by silt stirred up by the detonations. But Bikini's life system clearly was in a process of healing. Large islands were covered by regrowths of vegetation; on some, the masses of morning glory, beach magnolia and pandanus were growing so densely that field parties had extreme difficulty cutting paths through them. Bikini Atoll, scientists believed, needed only clearing and cultivation to make it once again suitable for human habitation.

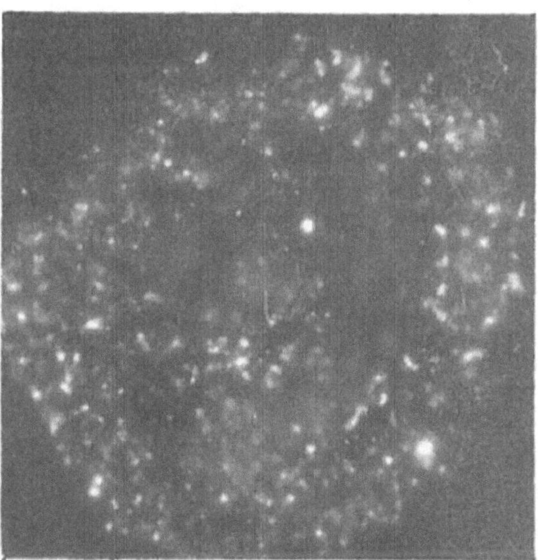

Autoradiograph of a plankton sample collected from a Pacific lagoon a week after a 1952 test.

[8] A thermonuclear device is an explosive, such as a hydrogen bomb, based on a fusion reaction. In other atomic weapons the energy is derived from nuclear fission.

What, then, may be concluded from the Bikini case? A final answer still cannot be phrased. It is not a conclusion to say that nature and time have permitted recovery, reassuring though such knowledge may be. It becomes important to know the processes of recovery. Meantime, it is helpful to examine the Bikini case in the context of developments during the period from the end of World War II to the signing of the Nuclear Test Ban Treaty of 1963.

THE BIKINI TESTS OF 1946

The early period of nuclear testing in the atmosphere was a time that will not be seen again. It was the beginning of an era of unparalleled scientific activity and of worldwide emotional and intellectual adjustment to the knowledge that power of unimaginable magnitude, locked in the nucleus of the atom since the creation of the world, now could be released at will.

When World War II was ended, the impulse to test the new power was irresistible. There was profound curiosity about the revolutionary nature of the new force. There was a perplexed and fearful realization that the release of energy would have to be guarded and controlled. There was the knowledge that nuclear fission produced a miscellany of radioactive products presenting unexplored possibilities of hazard. The word "fallout" was coined to describe the deposition on the earth of radioactive debris from nuclear explosions.

Joint Task Force One

The first peacetime nuclear tests, conducted at Bikini in 1946 in a military-scientific exercise designated Operation Crossroads, were designed to assess the effects of nuclear weapons on naval vessels. The test organization, Joint Task Force One, an adaptation of the wartime joint task force combat concept, was a massive waterborne force including 42,000 members of the armed services, civilian scientists, consultants, and observers.

The Bikini Lagoon before testing.

Bikini Atoll was selected for the tests because, among other things, it was remote from heavily populated areas, it offered a protected anchorage, and it had the relatively stable and predictable meteorological and oceanographic conditions considered essential to operations in which the unknowns loomed so large. Three test detonations originally were projected; two ultimately were carried out. The first, Test Able, was an airdrop of an atomic bomb on July 1, 1946, over a test fleet of 70 ships anchored in Bikini Lagoon. The second, Test Baker, was the detonation on July 25 of an atomic device suspended in the lagoon 90 feet below a small target vessel.

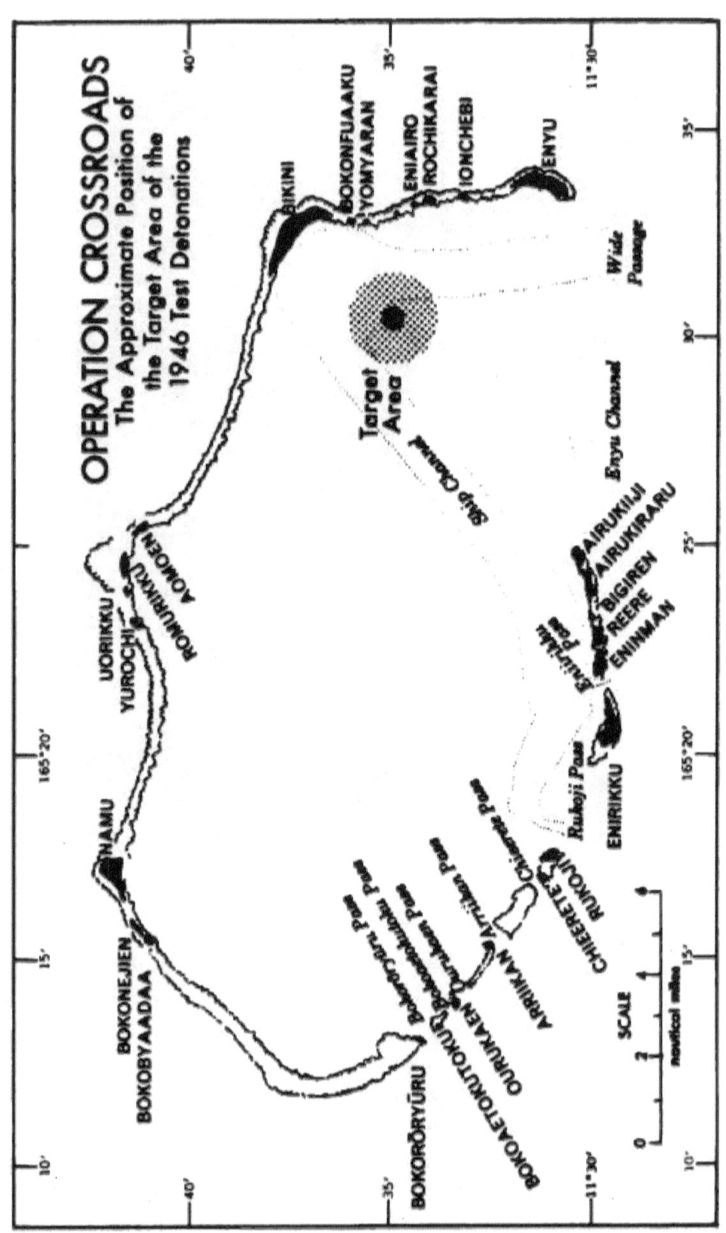

Scientific Interests

Although Crossroads was a military program, the mobilization of scientific interests was in many ways of historic proportions. For months before the explosions, oceanographers studied the waters and the structure of the mid-Pacific basin and meteorologists the winds and upper airs. Geologists, zoologists, botanists, and other specialists examined the atoll in detail. Bikini became, as it remains to this day, one of the most thoroughly familiar ocean structures in the world.

There was awareness, even then, of the significance of radioactivity as an element of nuclear effect. The task force made elaborate preparations to assure the safety of personnel and sent to the atoll thousands of radiation-detection instruments. Plans were made to observe the effects of radioactivity on test animals placed on ships of the target fleet.

The Underwater Detonation

The first of the Bikini events, Test Able, the explosion of a bomb dropped from an aircraft over the target fleet, sank a number of major vessels, left others sinking or crippled, contaminated many with radiation, and laid a plume of fallout northward over the rim of the atoll into the waters of the ocean. It was Test Baker, however, the underwater explosion, that would make Bikini the subject of radiobiological investigations for many years.

The Baker test was the first occasion in which nuclear debris was mixed with water and ocean sludge and returned to the area of detonation. The explosive device was of what later would be called nominal size, its force equivalent to 20,000 tons of TNT. The test still is regarded as a classic demonstration of the phenomena of shallow-water atomic explosion.

The Baker Test. A cauliflower-shaped cloud, after dumping one million tons of water that had been sucked up by the explosion, rises over the target warships, silhouetted in front of the spreading base surge.

At the moment of release, the surface water of the lagoon was first lifted and then penetrated by a lighted bubble that vanished in seconds in a hollow column of water of gigantic dimensions—a column 2000 feet in diameter (its walls 300 feet thick) rising to a height of 6000 feet and containing 1,000,000 tons of water. At the base of the column, foam was churned upward for several hundred feet, and, moving out from the base, as the column sank back into the lagoon, surged a monstrous wave initially more than 80 feet high.

Radioactivity in the water was intense. The immediate total was described as equal to "many hundred tons of radium". Decay and dilution of radioactive materials quickly reduced the total radioactivity. After 3 days, by which time water contamination had spread over an area of 50 square miles, the dose rate from the water was well within safe limits for persons remaining for brief periods. Yet it was several more days before inspection and scientific parties could spend useful time among the surviving target vessels.

At the bottom of the lagoon, below the point of detonation, Navy divers months later found that the explosion had scooped out thousands of tons of mud and coral sediment, creating a shallow basin half a mile wide. This basin, in the slow settling of returning sludge, became an area from which long-lived radioactivity entered Bikini's biological system.

First Assessments

In 3 weeks of final work after Test Baker, the Bikini scientific teams took from the islands and the lagoon many hundreds of samples of plants, corals, crabs, fish, plankton, and water. They noted that radioactivity was present in all samples taken from every part of the atoll, which indicated an early uptake of radionuclides by the biota[9] and suggested that there was a continuing circulation of radioactive debris in the water. They took samples of fish in the open ocean outside the atoll and made comparative collections at other atolls. The instruments and techniques for analyzing radioactivity were far from refined, but all available evidence pointed to the need for more particular efforts to examine radiobiological results.

THE BIKINI RESURVEY OF 1947

A resurvey of Bikini, the first of many, was conducted with heavy radioenvironmental emphasis in July 1947, a year after the Crossroads tests. The scientific expedition was supported by 2 vessels and included 70 scientists and several hundred Navy personnel.

---

[9] The living organisms.

Bikini Beach as it appeared in the years after Operation Crossroads.

The resurvey group, entering an oceanic environment that had been completely undisturbed for nearly a year, established at once that traces of residual radioactivity still were cycling in Bikini's ecosystem. For 6 weeks the scientists probed every realm of the atoll environment, sampling biota, making inventories of plant and animal communities, and obtaining core samples from the lagoon floor. When the data had been assembled and reviewed and the reports filed, months later, there was consensus that Bikini had produced no evidence that radioactivity, as a separate and identifiable factor, was having any immediate effect on the health of the atoll, and probably no cumulative effect, either.

There were, of course, unknowns. So long as radioactivity remained in the biological cycles there were possibilities of future developments. In 1947 no other place on earth offered an opportunity to observe the natural processes by which radiation contamination is eliminated from an environment. It therefore seemed prudent to compile a longer record, consisting of other, purely radiobiological surveys at Bikini.

By 1947 the new U. S. Atomic Energy Commission had taken over from the wartime Manhattan Engineering District the management of the national effort in the field of atomic energy. A primary responsibility of the AEC in that period was to press ahead with nuclear weapons development, but the agency also had specific obligations and interests in the fields of biology and medicine. Meantime, the testing of nuclear weapons had been started at a new proving ground at Eniwetok

Atoll, 190 nautical miles west of Bikini.

Islands on the rim of Eniwetok Atoll, as they appear today. The marks of man, such as a landing strip, are visible, but regrowth of vegetation is apparent. Note extent of the reef on both sides of islands.

STUDIES AT NUCLEAR TEST SITES, 1948-1958

The first test series at Eniwetok, Operation Sandstone (1948), incorporated no formal radiobiological studies, but radiobiologists visiting Bikini also made surveys at Eniwetok in 1948 and 1949. Then, for a time, world events intervened. The detonation of an atomic device by the U.S.S.R. in 1949 was followed in 1950 by the outbreak of the Korean War, and these events produced a national mood oriented toward national defense. By 1951, because events in the Pacific had interrupted tests there, the Atomic Energy Commission had established a continental test site in Nevada. In that year, too, tests were made at Eniwetok preliminary to the detonation of the first thermonuclear device.

After 1951 each of the test programs had its radiobiological component. In the Pacific, radiobiological surveys were associated with Operation Ivy (1952), Operation Castle (1954), Operation Redwing (1956), and Operation Hardtack (1958). A small field station, the Eniwetok Marine Biology Laboratory, was established for use by scientists conducting biological studies. Bikini was incorporated into the Pacific Proving Ground in 1953, and new biological surveys were performed there in connection with the tests of 1954 and later.

The Eniwetok Marine Biology Laboratory. Monument at right commemorates the battle for Eniwetok in World War II.

In these years, 1951 to 1958, the U.S.S.R. was testing nuclear weapons, as was Great Britain after 1952. Fallout from these contributed to the total of man-made radioactivity potentially available to the environments of the world.

LANDMARKS

The years between the establishment of the Pacific Proving Ground and the signing of the 1958 nuclear test moratorium were years in which the quest for environmental information could not keep pace with the rapid growth of nuclear capability. But the growth in the field of weapons served to underline the need for information and produced certain landmark developments in environmental research.

The detonation of the first thermonuclear device projected the problem of environmental contamination to the stratosphere and, literally, to every part of the earth. This explosion, Test Mike, largest on earth to that time, was set off on Elujelab Island, on the north rim of Eniwetok Atoll, on November 1, 1952. In the reef where Elujelab had been, the blast left a crater almost a mile in diameter and 200 feet deep. The towering nuclear cloud rose in 15 minutes to a height of 130,000 feet.

Test Mike marked a point of change. Before, fallout from nuclear detonation had been principally local, touching the waters and reefs of an atoll or a desert landscape. After Test Mike, the implications of fallout obviously were global.

A mishap in connection with a 1954 thermonuclear test at Bikini contributed in two important ways to the enlargement of environmental investigations. Fallout from the test, swept off its predicted pattern by unexpected winds at high altitudes, deposited debris on Rongelap, an inhabited atoll east of Bikini, and on fishermen aboard a Japanese vessel operating in the Bikini-Rongelap area. The accident, unfortunate in its consequences at Rongelap and in Japan, had other results of even wider impact. From it came the first international approaches to the problems of ocean contamination and, later, long-term bioenvironmental studies at Rongelap itself.

School of surgeonfish off Arji Island, Bikini Atoll, August 1964. Note coral growth on lagoon bottom.

Wide-ranging studies of ocean-borne radioactivity were initiated by the Japanese. The experience of the fishermen produced in Japan a fear of contamination of fisheries resources as a result of the United States tests. One result was the organization, in the summer of 1954, of a government-sponsored ocean survey expedition that cruised from Japan into and through the Bikini-Eniwetok area to determine what amounts of radioactivity were being carried, by water and by aquatic organisms, toward the shores of Japan.

The expedition made significant observations of the role of plankton[10] in the biological utilization of ocean fallout. A United States scientific team, following up the Japanese effort, made a similar but far more extensive cruise through the Western Pacific early in 1955 and went on to Japan to discuss its findings with the Japanese. During and after the test series in the Pacific in 1956 and 1958, United States surveys of the ocean were made routinely. Exchanges of information between scientists of Japan and the United States continued.

The Rongelap case produced results of another kind. The Rongelap people were found to have suffered exposure requiring medical attention and continued observation. Evacuated from their atoll because it was not safe, members of the

[10] Plankton are the floating, minute plants and animals that live in the sea (and also in fresh water), including diatoms, algae, protozoans, and crustaceans.

community were given care at other atolls until they could be repatriated in 1957, and received continued medical supervision thereafter.

The bioenvironmental condition of Rongelap was unique. The fallout had made the atoll the only place in the world contaminated on a single occasion by relatively heavy deposition of radioactive debris without also being disturbed by a nuclear explosion. In 1957-1958, after the Rongelapese had been returned to a new village constructed on their atoll, Rongelap was the site of a long and thorough study of the circulation of radionuclides in the terrestrial-aquatic environment.

BEFORE THE 1963 TEST BAN TREATY

The first break in the pattern of nuclear testing came in 1958, when the nuclear powers agreed to a 1-year test moratorium. The world's political and emotional climates were changing. For more than 5 years, the United States, which had announced its Atoms-for-Peace Program in December 1953, had been endeavoring to place emphasis on the use of atomic energy for constructive purposes. The Atomic Energy Act of 1954, liberalizing provisions of the 1946 law, contemplated for the first time private development of nuclear power resources and established authority for international activities. In 1957 the Atomic Energy Commission initiated its Plowshare Program for the development of peaceful uses of nuclear explosives.[11]

Amid such changes there was arising, too, a wider apprehension concerning the possible effects of fallout. The United Nations in 1955 appointed a committee of scientific representatives of 15 nations to study the effects of radiation on man. In the United States the National Academy of Sciences published in 1956 the first of its summary reports on the biological effects of atomic radiation.

Nuclear testing was not ended by the 1958 agreement, yet the moratorium—which was renewed annually until 1961, when the U.S.S.R. broke the agreement by initiating a new test series—was significant as an experiment in nuclear restraint. After the United States conducted a final test series near Christmas Island in 1962, new discussions of ways to halt successive rounds of nuclear test programs were held. Finally, in 1963, the Nuclear Test Ban Treaty was signed by most of the nations of the world. The treaty was, among other things, a declaration against worldwide fallout.

---

[11] For more on this program, see *Plowshare,* a companion booklet in this series.

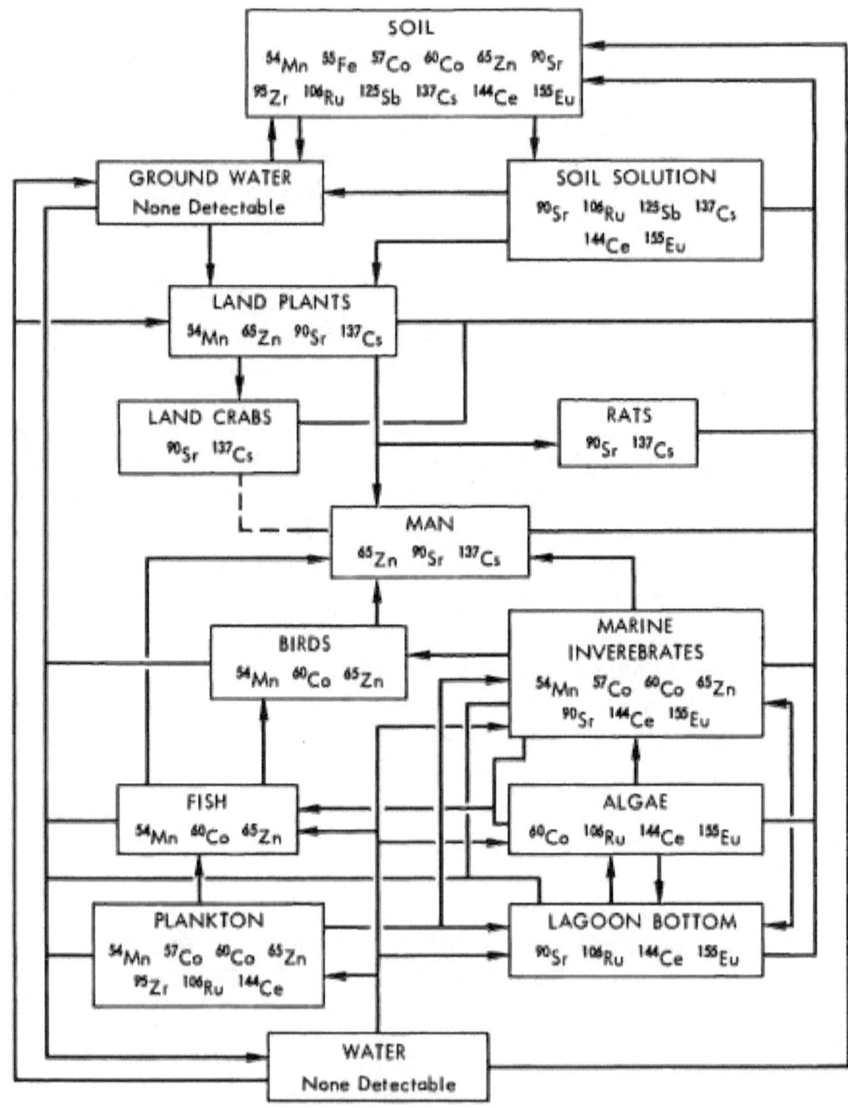

Distribution of fallout radioisotopes on Rongelap Atoll as determined by a survey in 1961. Note the interrelationships of man, plants, animals and the environment.

THE ATOM IN ENVIRONMENTAL STUDIES

Although his experience with radioactivity has been brief, man probably already knows more about the effects of radiation than he knows about the effects of many other contaminants that alter his environment. Even so, he knows far less than he needs to know to make certain that atomic energy is wisely managed in the future.

There has been neither time nor opportunity, for example, to gather radiation-effects data on more than a few hundred of the 1,500,000 kinds of living organisms inhabiting the earth. Nor is it possible to predict the extent to which life can adjust itself to environmental changes resulting from scarcely perceptible alterations of natural radiological balances. Also undetermined is the relation between environmental changes and the biological exchanges making up the often mentioned, but insufficiently understood, "balance of nature".

The case of carbon-14 is an example of a permanent man-made modification of the environment. From the early ages of the earth, carbon-14 has been created in the upper atmosphere by the transmutation of nitrogen in cosmic-ray reactions. Carbon itself is an almost universal component of living matter, and the ratio between stable carbon and radioactive carbon is believed to have been unchanged for thousands of years. It is this circumstance that permits the use of carbon-14 as a tool for "dating", or determining the ages of, fossil remains, prehistoric artifacts, and geologic formations. But carbon-14 also is produced in nuclear fusion, and the testing of thermonuclear devices after 1952 produced an estimated increase of 4% in the amount of carbon-14 on earth. This is enough to disturb the natural equilibrium. Since the half-life[12] of carbon-14 is some 5800 years, the addition will be a factor of environmental consideration for scores of human generations.

Nuclear tests, although not the only sources of man-made radioactivity, have been until now the most significant ones and the only sources touching large areas of the earth. The total product of nuclear testing is small in relation to the natural burden of radioactivity, raising the level of radiation to which all life is subject by a factor of one-tenth or less. But it is the unknown element, the degree to which fallout radioactivity may introduce new influences into the environment, that gives concern.[13]

---

[12] The half-life of a radioactive element is the time required for half its atoms to lose their radioactivity.

[13] Atmospheric tests of nuclear weapons through 1962 produced a fission yield equivalent to 191 million tons of TNT and introduced about 10.01 megacuries of strontium-90, for example, as fallout entering the environment.

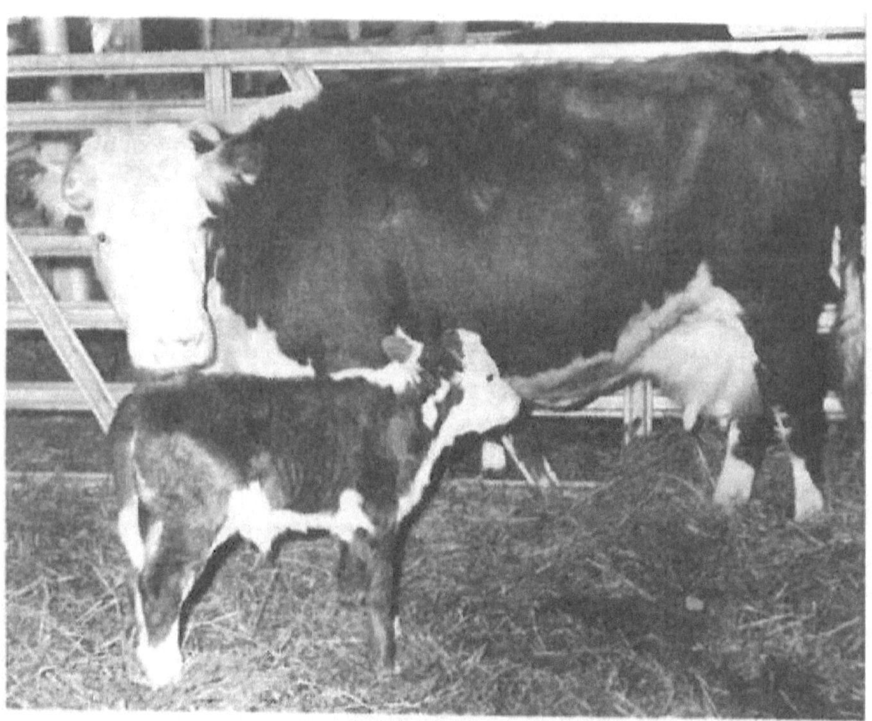

One of the last cows of the herd exposed to fallout by the world's first atomic detonation in New Mexico in July 1945, photographed in 1964. The calf is her 15th to be born in 15 years. The cow, believed about 20 years old, has been under observation by scientists, who found she suffered little apparent effect, although the fallout caused some hair to turn gray (see light patches on back). Other cows in the herd died natural deaths.

When a nuclear device is detonated, the release of energy is due to the fission of uranium or plutonium atoms or to the fusion of hydrogen atoms. At the instant of fission, some 75 radionuclides, or fission products, are created.

From these primary fission products, about 100 other radionuclides may be formed, some existing only for microseconds and others for thousands of years. The radionuclides of significance to biologists are those that exist long enough— no matter how brief the time—to have an impact on a biological system.

Factors of biological transport and concentration of long-lived radionuclides make efforts to assess possible environmental effects particularly difficult. It has been asserted, for example, that probably every living cell formed since the early 1950s contains some of the radionuclides produced by nuclear testing. No one knows the significance of such a condition, if it indeed exists. It is certain only that some of the long-lived radionuclides already placed in the environment will be detectable there for hundreds of years and hence will continue to provide material for biological studies.

EXAMINING ENVIRONMENTS

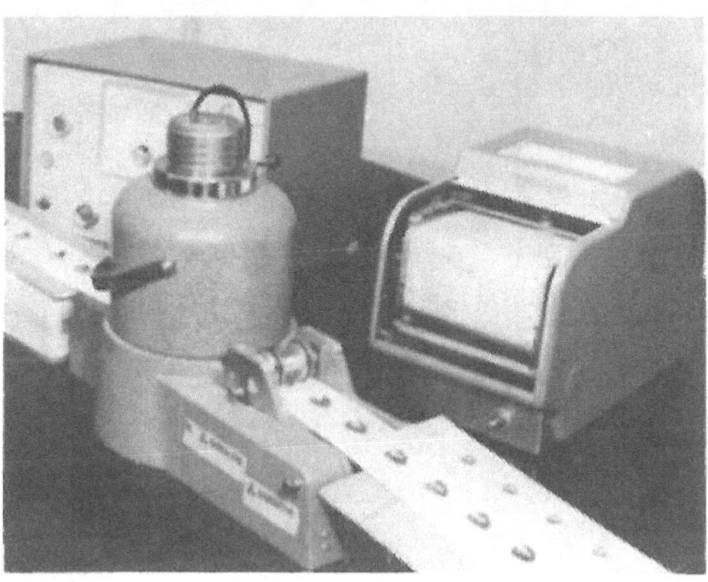

Seeds produced by plants grown in soil of a radioactive waste disposal area pass (in aluminum cups) on moving belt through a radioactivity detector as part of a study of movement of radioisotopes in food chains.

When radioactivity is injected randomly into the atmosphere by a nuclear detonation, biological disposition begins in many ways, each related to the character of the explosion and the environment in which it occurs. Fallout studies thus involve the tracing of mixed fission products in the biosphere and the collection and analysis of thousands of samples of plant and animal tissue, and usually of water and soils, at many successive times. The radiobiologist then attempts to interpret the accumulated evidence of uptake of radionuclides. Some fallout studies may require sampling over large areas of the earth. Other investigations of fallout or of radioisotopes introduced deliberately into controlled field plots may require years of patient observation in small and circumscribed areas.

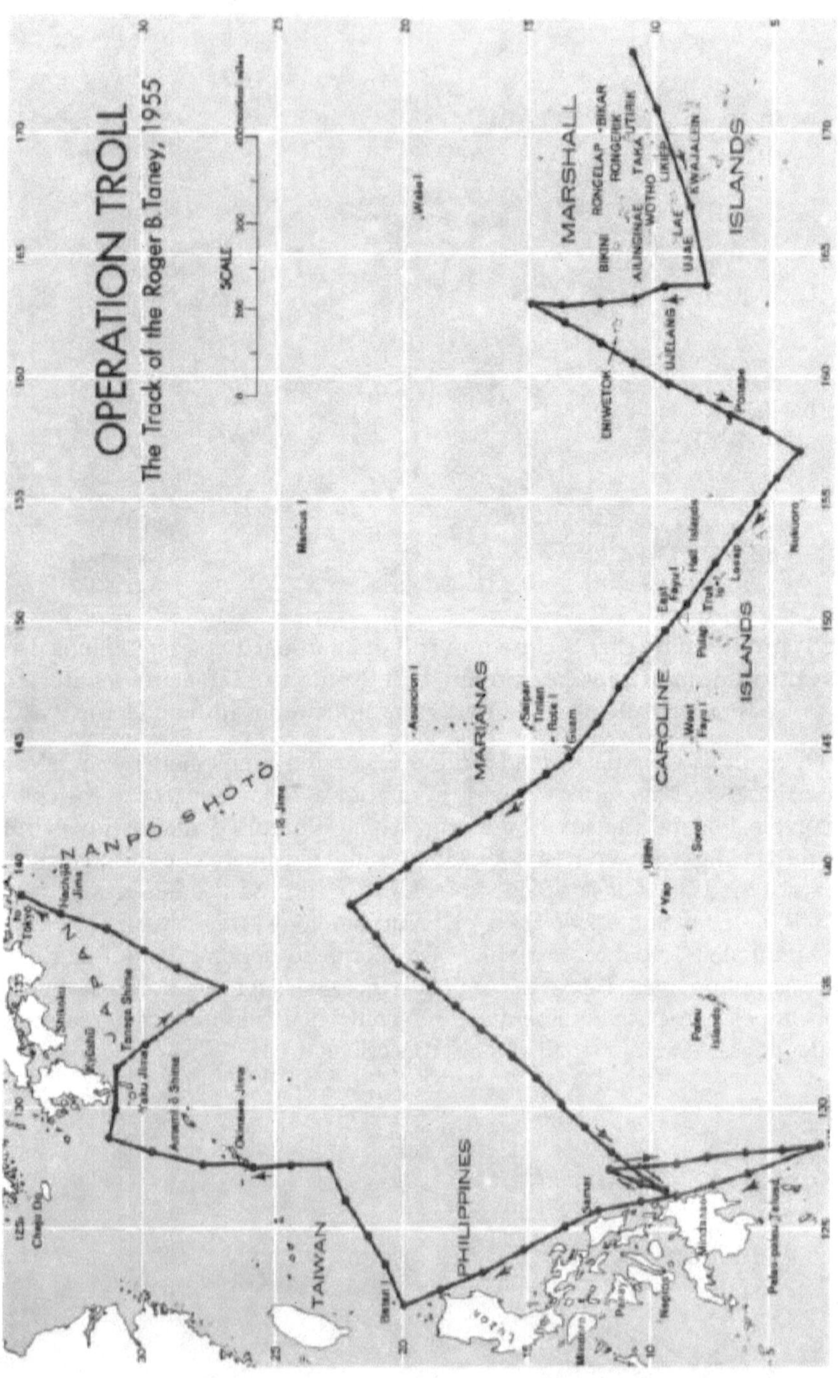

Studies of ocean fallout, for example, have ranged over hundreds of thousands of square miles of open water. The 1955 United States survey of the Western Pacific was conducted by a scientific team aboard a Coast Guard vessel, the *Roger B. Taney*, in a program called Operation Troll. In 7 weeks the team cruised 17,500 miles, making collections of water and marine organisms at 86 ocean stations on a route extending from the Marshall Islands through the Caroline Islands and the Mariana Islands to the Philippines and finally to Tokyo. The expedition took samples of plankton at depths down to 200 meters and water from the surface down to depths of 600, 800, 1000, and 1200 meters.

Environmental studies at nuclear test sites or in controlled ecosystems involve not only long-term, periodic sampling of plants and animals but also years of detailed examination of soils, meteorological conditions, and other factors.

TERRESTRIAL ECOLOGY RESEARCH

An ecologist inspects cages placed around bagworm infestations of a red cedar tree that had been injected with radioactive cesium-134 to determine uptake of radioactivity in the larvae.

Checking pine seedlings exposed to ionizing radiation from a radioactive source (on tripod) in a controlled ecosystem. Seedlings on left were fully exposed, those in the middle were exposed on their tops only, and those on the right were exposed on their stems only.

Biologist studying the root distribution of plants by injecting radionuclides into the soil and measuring plant uptake.

A thriving Messerschmidia plant growing on Rongelap Atoll is studied for growth-rate and root-systems data after the island was accidentally subjected to radioactive fallout.

Aerial view of a "Gamma Forest", where growing trees are exposed to chronic irradiation from a source at the center of the picture. This environmental biology study shows varying sensitivity of various trees. Trees in the center were killed by extremely high doses of radiation for 20 hours a day over a 6-month period.

Apparatus containing a strong radiation source being installed by biologists in a semitropical rain forest for terrestrial ecology research.

In programs of such scope and duration, the problems of interpretation are great. Broadly, environmental studies give consideration to:

1. The amounts and kinds of radioactivity released to the environment.

2. The rates of uptake by the biological system.

3. The amounts and kinds of radioactivity within the system.

4. The rates of metabolic transfer or elimination.

5. The amounts and kinds of radioactivity concentrated in tissue and acting internally.

6. The time required for biological processes to be completed and for any biological effects to develop.

BIOLOGICAL INVENTORIES

Familiarity with the biological components of an ecosystem is essential to meaningful radiobiological assessment.

Inventories of natural components were not made in the early nuclear test programs because of inadequate realization of the biological potential. Later, they could be made only after radionuclides already had been introduced into the environments.

The survey of the mid-Pacific region before Operation Crossroads represented the earliest effort to examine an environment in detail before a nuclear detonation, but was designed so that it had only inferential value for other long-range biological research. The test surveys were useful, however, in expanding knowledge of specific environments. In addition, it was standard practice to make comparative collections of organisms in regions removed from the test sites to establish base lines, or "controls", against which to measure radiobiological developments.

The most extensive inventory of an environment—an inventory designed specifically in relation to an anticipated nuclear detonation—was that made between 1959 and 1962, as a preliminary phase of Project Chariot, in the Cape Thompson area of Northwest Alaska. Chariot was a part of the AEC Plowshare Program in which it was proposed to excavate a harbor at the mouth of the Ogotoruk Creek, which empties into the Chukchi Sea. Although the excavation project actually never was undertaken, the "predetonation" environmental investigations involved 3 years of coordinated research into the climatic, marine, coastal, and terrestrial aspects of the region, and detailed studies of the history and the radiological and ecological situations of the human population.

Taking a soil sample for the Project Chariot biological inventory to determine kinds and relative abundance of invertebrates and other soil organisms.

The program was an effort to make a model environmental inventory. Its significance was both in its assessment of the base for determining the "biological cost" of the proposed operation and in the thoroughness of its documentation of the environmental features of a part of the world that previously had been virtually unexplored. It was a prototype for future studies.

MEASUREMENTS AND INTERPRETATIONS

Determination of the amounts and kinds of radioactivity in a biological sample is a process wholly dependent on instruments, since radiation usually cannot be detected by the senses.

A biological sample is any material of measurable biological significance. A sample of tissue or similar organic material usually is dried or reduced to ash in a muffle furnace before it is examined with a radiation counting device.

Improved instruments now permit the counting of radioactivity at levels so low as to have been imperceptible a few years ago. The samples, placed in lead chambers for maximum shielding from background radiations, are examined by multichannel analyzers capable of recording radiation emissions continuously over long periods of time.

Data-processing techniques have been employed in the handling and interpretation of information from long-range biological sampling and analysis programs. Analog computers have been used experimentally for theoretical projections of results.

Instruments record radiation, weather, sunlight, and other factors transmitted from remote sensors to this data center established for a long-range terrestrial ecology study program.

Scientists at the AEC's Oak Ridge National Laboratory, for example, have developed experiments in which an analog computer is programmed to keep a running balance of the net changes—simultaneous gains and losses—of radioactivity in the various compartments of a representative ecosystem. The computer becomes an electronic image of the biosphere, using known or assumed rates of energy transfer and photosynthesis to predict probable radiological results of tracer experiments of environmental contamination.

ENVIRONMENTS—SINGULAR, YET PARTS OF A WHOLE

Each environment presents its own sets of conditions and unknowns. It is important to appreciate those that are characteristic of water, land, and atmosphere.

AQUATIC SYSTEMS

The oceans are the basins into which are poured all the nutrients or wastes transported from the land by rivers and winds.

The difficulty of determining the fate of radionuclides in aquatic systems is complicated by chemical and biological differences within the system and by the variety and scope of the circulatory mechanisms. In oceans the sheer immensity of the water volume usually makes observation superficial or fragmentary. Rivers present great differences in flow, and lakes vary in internal dynamics. Above all, an ocean, a river, or a lake is an area of constant physical and biological motion and change. In the ocean the surface waters form a theater of kaleidoscopic, and frequently violent, action. The presence of man-made radioactivity in water has made it possible to follow the disposition of nutrients and wastes in the restless aquatic ecosystem.

Biological Uptake

In a water environment the minerals necessary to life are held in solution or lie in bottom sediments. They become available to animal life after being absorbed by plants, both large floating or rooted plants and tiny floating ones called phytoplankton; because the phytoplankton are found everywhere in the sea, they play a larger role. The phytoplankton concentrate minerals and become food for filter-feeding fish and other creatures, including the smaller zooplankton,[14] which, in turn, are food for other organisms. Thus the minerals enter extremely complex food chains. The cycles of nutrition are completed when fish and plants die and decomposition again makes the minerals available to the phytoplankton.

---

[14] Floating one-celled animals.

ENVIRONMENTAL RESEARCH

RAIN FOREST. A giant fan pulls air through a plastic-enclosed portion of a Puerto Rico rain forest to study the metabolism rate of trees.

HARDWOOD FOREST. Technicians preparing to tag Tennessee trees with a solution containing a radioactive cesium isotope in the start of a 10-year project. Scientists will study movement of the radioactivity into insects and their predators.

FRESHWATER. Aquatic biologists emptying plankton traps to study concentrations of radioactivity in microscopic organisms in the Columbia River downstream from the Hanford atomic plant in Washington State.

MOUNTAINS. Weather station in a deer-forage area of the Rocky Mountains in Colorado provides environmental data and fallout samples that are correlated with levels of radionuclides found in the deer.

TUNDRA. This caribou was examined in detail as part of a study of transfer of fallout nuclides in food chains from plants to animals to man. Caribou is the principal meat animal of some Alaska Eskimos.

DESERT. Zoologist examines an animal trap as part of a field ecological study of a Nevada nuclear test site.

Some radionuclides that are introduced into an aquatic environment enter the food chains exactly as do the stable minerals essential to life, because the radio-nuclides are merely radioactive forms of the nutrients. Elements such as copper, zinc, and iron are less plentiful in the water environment than hydrogen, carbon, or oxygen, for example, but are concentrated by phytoplankton because they are necessary for life. Such elements are in short supply but in constant demand; thus, when their radioactive forms are deposited in water, they are immediately taken up by aquatic plants and begin to move through the food chains. Fission products such as strontium-90, for which there is little or no metabolic demand, are taken up by aquatic food chains to only a minor extent.

The precise paths of radioelements through aquatic ecosystems are almost un-known. In addition to their movement in food chains, radioelements also may be moved physically from place to place in the tissues of fish or other creatures. Some radionuclides for which there is no biological demand may sink into bottom sed-iments and remain there until they have lost their radioactivity. Or radioactivity actually may be transported "uphill", from water to land, as when birds that feed on fish containing radioactivity leave their excretions at nesting areas. The routes and modes of transport seem numberless.

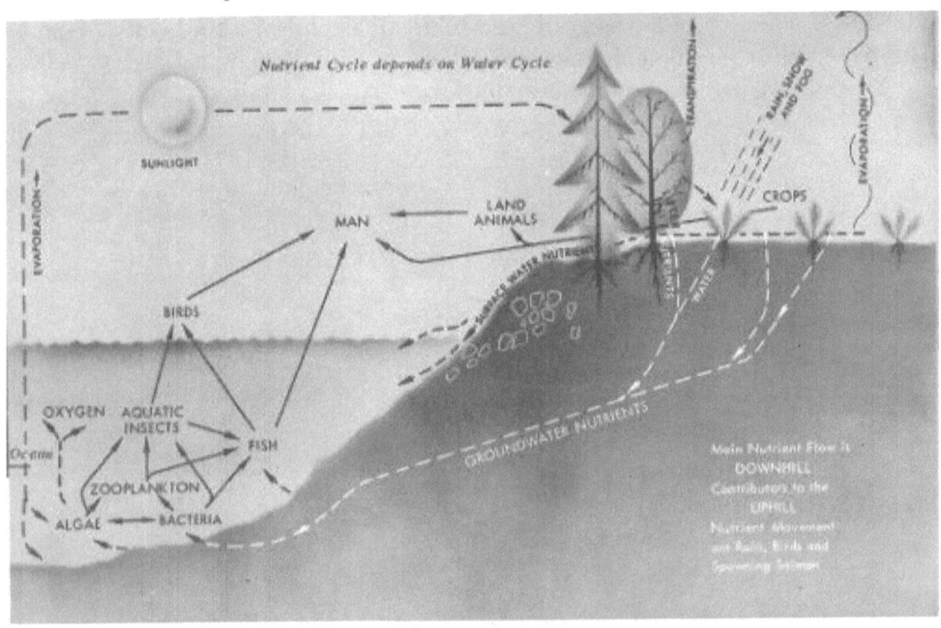

Movement of radioactive elements in a forest-lake ecological system. Most nu-trient-flow is "downhill", but birds, migrating fish, and the evaporation-rain-fall cycle may move them "uphill".

The Oceans

The surface waters of the seas, down to depths of 200 meters, are areas of rapid mixing in which temperature, density, and salinity are almost uniform. Below the surface water is a zone in which temperature decreases and density and salinity increase with depth. This zone, known as the thermocline, may reach a depth of 1000 meters. Because density is increasing here, vertical motion is reduced, and exchanges between the surface and the deep waters are impeded. Knowledge of temperature, density, and salinity is important to understanding what happens to radionuclides in the ocean. Physical conditions affect the rates of physical movement of radioactivity in the mixed (surface) layer, the degree to which radionuclides are held at the thermocline, and the processes by which radionuclides pass the thermocline and enter the deep-water cycles and upwellings.

Men aboard the research vessel Shimada pulling in plankton nets during sampling operations at sea.

The surface currents of the ocean are largely wind driven and their patterns generally well known. New concepts of the vertical and horizontal diffusion of substances introduced into the ocean were developed, however, in studies of ocean-borne fallout during and after nuclear tests in the Pacific.

The first of these surveys was conducted near Eniwetok and Bikini. Scientists aboard a Navy vessel sampled water and plankton to depths of 300 meters at some 90 points spread over an area of 78,000 square miles to determine the disposition of early fallout from the nuclear detonations. Some weeks later another expedition voyaged from Eniwetok to Guam and returned, covering an area of 375,000 square miles to follow (by sampling) the mass of water-borne radioactivity resulting from the test and to note the intervening effects of diffusion, dilution, biological uptake, and decay. In 1958 two more surveys were conducted, the first to ascertain the spread and depth—with samplings below the thermocline—of a radioactively tagged water mass immediately following an underwater detonation, and the second to follow the westward drift of the tagged water mass.

Significantly, it was found that plankton immediately take up large amounts of radioactivity. Planktonic forms, in fact, proved to be the most sensitive indicators of the presence of radioactivity in the marine environment. Further, the daily vertical migrations of plankton—down in response to sunlight and up at night—seemed a part of the process by which radionuclides move from the upper waters to the deeps.

The expedition scientists noted that the masses of low-level radioactivity moved in the ocean significantly slower than the surface currents, a circumstance attributable in large measure to biological factors. The distribution of residual radioactivity in the sea a month after the close of a nuclear testing program could be determined by counting radioactivity in plankton samples.

It was established that strontium-90 and cesium-137, important in fallout on land, enter the marine cycles only in minute amounts. Practically no fission products are found in fish. Since strontium-90 is not concentrated strongly by marine organisms, the question of what happens to it in the ocean remains unanswered. Studies have suggested, however, that strontium moves in solution and thus indicates the movement of water. If this is true, strontium-90 may be contained in the deep currents and eventually will be brought again to the surface. Some observers believe this process has begun.

Rivers, Lakes, and Estuaries

The freshwater environment differs from the marine in the greater variety of its minerals, among other things. As sites for radiobiological studies, rivers and lakes present problems of great complexity, but conditions at river mouths or estuaries are even more difficult because of the mixing by tidal action of fresh and salt water.

Rivers vary greatly in character and change radically from season to season because of rainfall and other factors. General understanding of their biological workings is difficult to formulate. But rivers are the routes by which minerals and wastes are transported toward the sea, and estuaries are significant because of the many forms of life that flourish there.

Studies of radioactivity in rivers and estuaries usually have been made in relation to the fate of effluents from nuclear plants. Among the longest and most intensive studies are those near Hanford, Washington. Observations were started in 1943, when the federal government was preparing to build plutonium-producing reactors to be cooled by waters of the Columbia River.

Fisheries biologists studying hatchery fish reared in water containing radioactivity from the Hanford plutonium reactors.

For more than two decades, observations have been made of the physical dispersion and biological disposition of low-level effluents in the Columbia. Concentration factors have been established for significant radionuclides in phytoplankton, algae, insects, and fish, and typical patterns of dilution and dispersion have been plotted.

Similar programs, in an entirely different freshwater system, have been conducted over a similar span of years near the Oak Ridge National Laboratory in Tennessee. One area of interest has been the biological disposition of trace amounts of strontium-90 released to the Tennessee River via tributary streams.

Among the few broad estuarial studies yet undertaken is one started in 1961 to plot the dissemination in the lower Columbia River, and in the Pacific Ocean, of radioisotopes transported by the river from the Hanford plant. Radiobiologists are studying biological distribution. Oceanographers are using the trace amounts of effluent radioactivity to verify the patterns of dispersion of river waters in the ocean.

LAND

Plant ecologists "tagging" experimental forest plots with radioactive cesium for long-term studies.

Natural radionuclides find their way into plants' metabolic processes. Man-made radionuclides also are so incorporated—even some, such as uranium or radium, that have no known metabolic role. The man-made nuclides, whether they reach the earth in fallout or by other means, mix with the stable nuclides to which they are chemically related, increasing by small fractions the total amount of each element available to participate in plant growth cycles. Because artificial radionuclides behave so typically, they present, on the one hand, a possible long-term hazard and, on the other, the expectation that their detectability will reveal much about the biological courses of minerals and nutrients.

The disposition of man-made radioactivity on land is determined in part by such factors as topography and the presence or absence of water. Topography may influence the distribution by setting patterns of drainage and exposure of surface soils to wind and rain. Water may affect dilution, or it may leach radionuclides out of surface soils and thus remove them from the level in which plants are rooted. The leaching may carry radionuclides elsewhere, however, possibly causing mild contamination of the water table.

Trench dug on Rongelap Island to expose soil strata and root systems to determine penetration of radionuclides in coral-sand "topsoil".

Plants take up radionuclides through their roots or through their foliage. But the role of soils is significant. Some radionuclides are bound as ions to clays and thus are withheld in large measure from entry into the plant system. Cesium-137, for example, is held so tightly by soils that uptake through plant roots is slight, and thus a more significant mode of entry of cesium-137 into food chains is by direct deposit on plant leaves. Variables are introduced by the physical configuration of the plant itself, by seasonal differences in plant metabolism, and by the effects of rain and snow. In the case of iodine-131, a short half-life—8 days—virtually precludes the possibility of extensive uptake through plant roots. But the half-life is not too short to prevent grazing cattle from ingesting radioiodine deposited in fallout and thus allow the appearance of radioiodine in milk.

Survey of pasture grasses to determine whether radioactive materials are present. If they are, they could be passed from the grasses to cows and then from the cows' milk to humans.

Much attention has been devoted to strontium-90 and to its availability to man by deposit on plants and soils. Because strontium bears a close chemical relation to calcium, a unit expressing this relation, the *strontium unit* (one picocurie[15] [1 × 10^{-12} curie of strontium-90 per gram of calcium]) is used in following strontium-90 through food chains. Soils, however, present confusing factors. Experiments and fallout observations show that strontium-90 does not penetrate soils deeply. In typical instances it remains in the upper inch or two of the soil surface, where its availability to root systems is as variable as the conditions of mixing, leaching, and plant growth. Experiments have shown that plant uptake of strontium from soils can be reduced by introduction of calcium in available form into the soil.

Radiobiological developments on land result from combinations of environmental influences. Studies in the Rocky Mountains show that ecological conditions above the timberline, particularly in areas where snowbanks accumulate, are efficient in concentrating fallout radionuclides. Concentrations thus take place in the snow-packed heights that are the sources of mountain streams flowing to the

[15] A picocurie is one trillionth of a curie; a curie is the basic unit of intensity of radioactivity, approximately equal to that in 1 gram of radium.

plains far below.

ATMOSPHERE

The environment of the earth is a product of "weather"—of the transport of moisture, of the actions between winds and oceans, of the cycling of energy through biotic systems. Understanding of biological potentials of atmospheric factors involves understanding of atmospheric motions affecting transport and mixing of contaminants and the processes of deposition of radionuclides from atmosphere to earth.

Network of towers on the Atomic Energy Commission reservation near Richland, Washington, used by atmospheric physicists in measuring quantity, concentration, and dilution of radioactive materials in the atmosphere.

At some thousands of feet above the earth's surface—at 30,000 to 40,000 feet in the middle and polar latitudes and at 50,000 to 60,000 feet in the tropics—there is a level, the tropopause, at which air temperature, rather than decreasing, becomes constant or increases with height. Below this level is the troposphere, the turbulent zone of clouds, rain, and fog. Above it is the stratosphere, where there is no turbulence and only a slow mixing of dry and cloudless air. The stratosphere continues to a height of about 100,000 feet. Investigators have noted the importance of rain or snow in washing fallout particles from the air in the troposphere. There is disagreement on the precise modes of distribution of radioactive materials projected into the stratosphere.

In the detonation of low-yield nuclear devices, fission products are not projected beyond the troposphere, and fallout is washed down in periods of days or weeks. Because winds move principally in east-west directions, tropospheric fallout appears on the earth in bands centered approximately at the latitude of detonation. But when high-yield explosions propel contaminants into the stratosphere, the pattern of subsequent developments is less clear. It once was believed that fallout from the stratosphere was distributed more or less evenly—though over long periods of time—over the surface of the earth. The present view is that fallout debris placed in the stratosphere remains in that hemisphere in which the explosion occurs. This concept is based on an atmospheric circulation theory that air enters the stratosphere at the equator and descends again in temperate and polar latitudes each spring. The theory presumes a much shorter "residence time" of stratospheric air and thus a quicker return of fallout particles to the turbulent troposphere.[16]

The presence of radionuclides in the atmosphere has provided clues to cyclical movements of biological importance. During the period of nuclear tests in the Pacific, observers noted spring "pulses", or increases, of strontium-90 deposition in the northern hemisphere, a phenomenon difficult to verify or explain satisfactorily while testing was proceeding. Later, when testing had been suspended, the spring peaks reappeared. The observation seemed to support the theory that nuclear debris injected into the stratosphere was descending years later through a gap in the tropopause.

Samplings of nuclear debris by balloon have been under way for several years at altitudes of 100,000 to 150,000 feet, and rocket-borne air samplers and other systems have been developed for taking atmospheric samples up to 200,000 feet.

Programs for studying airborne contamination from industrial activities—operated at the more accessible but equally difficult levels of the atmosphere—have been sponsored by the Atomic Energy Commission near the Hanford Plant, Washington, and at the Oak Ridge, Argonne, and Brookhaven National Laboratories in Tennessee, Illinois, and New York. The Hanford studies were started before plutonium production was begun in 1943, and findings on industrial stack-discharge rates established patterns for meteorological programs at other sites.[17]

---

[16] For more about these studies, see *Fallout from Nuclear Weapons Tests*, a companion booklet in this series.

[17] Information on this research is found in *Radioactive Wastes*, a companion booklet in this series.

PROBLEMS AND PROJECTS

The range and variety of environmental studies now in progress make it almost impossible to provide any all-encompassing statement of results. Almost all places associated with nuclear programs have become focal points of research in environmental biology. Fallout, deposited in patterns determined by the mechanisms of the atmosphere, has created at certain points on the earth's surface—the Arctic, for example—ecological conditions that require investigation. New information of bioenvironmental significance has come in bits and fragments. We can, however, attempt to summarize what has been learned and to show, in broad terms, how radiobiological experience has extended appreciation of the earth as a single ecosystem—a system comprised of an infinity of interactions of water, land, and atmosphere, and of all living things.

The spectrum of environmental investigation—investigations using man-made radioactivity—incorporates research in which:

1. Fallout radioactivity is assessed as a potential specific hazard to human populations.

2. Conditions created by fallout are examined for their potential long-term ecological significance.

3. Radionuclides introduced into the environment by nuclear tests, reactor operations, or other means are used as trace materials in basic studies in biological systems.

4. Radioactive forms of minerals and nutrients are deliberately introduced into biosystems—in measured amounts and under conditions of control—for studies of metabolic cycles and rates of flow of energy and nutrition.

It will be useful to look in detail at some typical programs and results.

ANIMAL RESEARCH

RAT. A lightly anesthetized, wild trapped rat is weighed and measured prior to marking it, taking a blood sample, and releasing it in a controlled ecosystem.

FISH. Fisheries biologist with a large jackfish caught off Engebi Island, Eniwetok Atoll.

COCONUT CRAB. Measuring the radioactivity of the shell of a coconut crab caught on Bikini Island.

GEESE. Banding wild geese to study environmental effects of radionuclides on wildlife and possible entry of radionuclides into the human food chain.

PLANKTON. An ingenious plankton trap is placed in a river as part of a long-range study of radionuclide uptake by aquatic organisms.

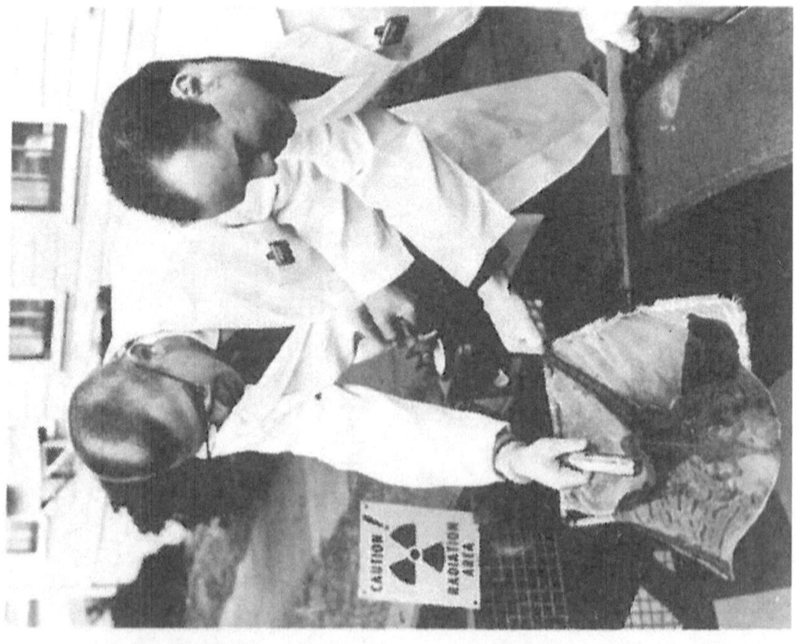

SKATE. A clear-nosed skate being monitored by fisheries personnel to gather data on accumulation of radionuclides in its blood and tissues.

WASPS AND RADIOACTIVE MUD

At Oak Ridge National Laboratory, Tennessee, it was discovered in 1964 that two kinds of mud-dauber wasps were building their mud nests in equipment, cabinets, and electronic gear in the vicinity of a field station on the Oak Ridge reservation.

Some nests, investigation disclosed, were built of radioactive mud. It seemed obvious that the wasps were obtaining mud from radioactive waste pits or from the White Oak Lake bed, which is the site of a former 40-acre lake used for 12 years as a detention pool for radioactive wastes.[18]

The mud daubers were carrying mud as far as 650 feet from the contaminated sources. Almost 90% of 112 nests built by the yellow-legged mud-dauber species were radioactive, and the mud was delivering to the wasp eggs each hour a dose of penetrating radiation equal to that received by a man from all natural sources over a period of many years. The development presented no human health problems, but further observation revealed a fascinating circumstance.

At the same time, another variety of wasp, the pipe-organ mud dauber, was building nests only of *non*radioactive mud. Of 150 pipe-organ wasp nests examined, none was radioactive. The nests were found in similar locations, and it was apparent that the same sources of nest materials were available to both species.

---

[18] The lake, drained in 1955, makes an interesting natural basin in which residual radionuclides are used in studies of mineral cycling.

WASP NEST RESEARCH

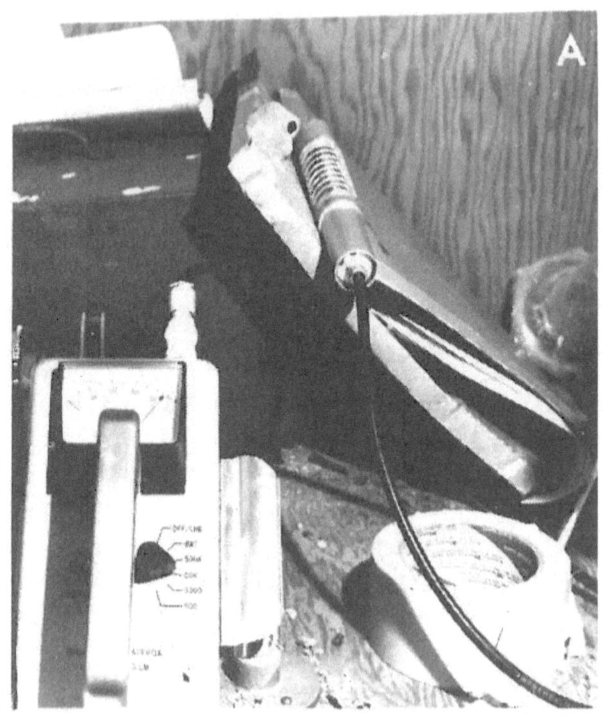

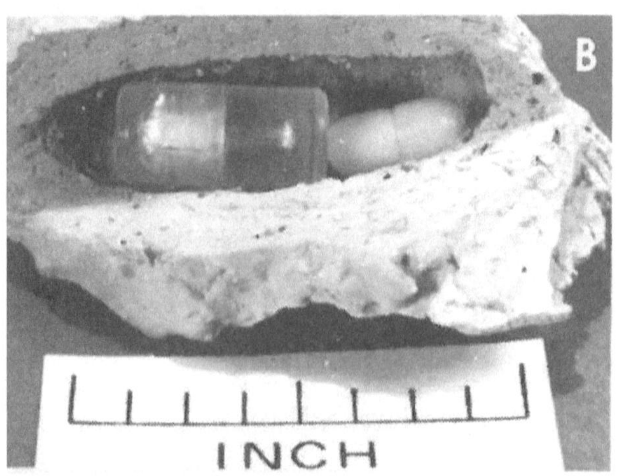

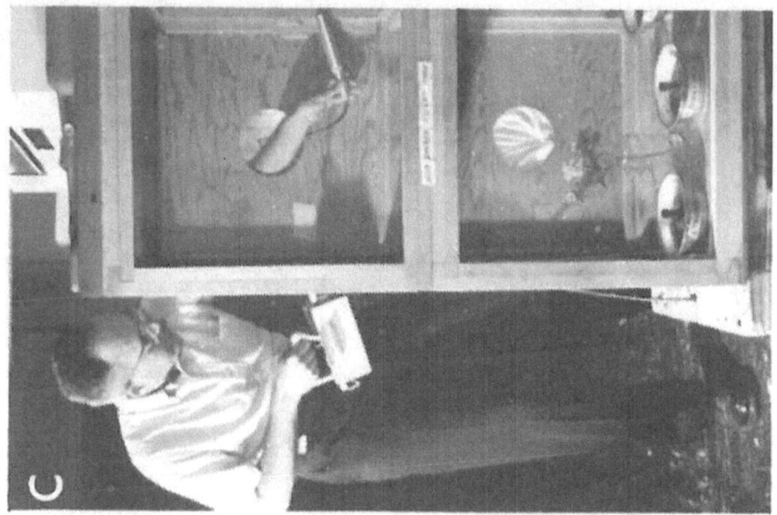

Mud-dauber wasps, building nests of radioactive mud in a waste disposal area near an Oak Ridge, Tennessee, atomic plant, are the object of intensive environmental radiation study. A shows radioactivity reading from a nest. B is an enlarged view of the nest with two tiny dosimeters in place to measure radiation. In C an ecologist inspects new nests built in a laboratory flight cage from radioactive mud provided in pans at the bottom. In D wasps are anesthetized, marked with tiny plastic disks for future identification, and released.

The question, then, was why wasps of one species were using radioactive mud while the other species seemingly discriminated against contaminated mud. The muds appeared to be entirely alike. X-ray-diffraction studies showed no material differences, nor were there detectable differences in "feel", smell, or plasticity. Radioactive isotopes in the mud included cesium-137, cobalt-60, ruthenium-106, and zinc-65. Oak Ridge scientists began to try to find out whether the pipe-organ wasps actually were discriminating against muds containing all or some of these radioisotopes or against the ionizing radiation from them. If so, how could the wasps detect it? These investigations were continuing in 1965. There is no answer yet.

SURVIVAL OF AN ANIMAL POPULATION

The case of Bikini already has been discussed as an example of a predominantly aquatic environment apparently recovering from association with nuclear experiment. Eniwetok offers an instance of the toughness of an animal population exposed both to direct and long-range radiological impact.

Engebi Island, on Eniwetok's northeast reef, is the home of a wholly self-contained colony of Pacific rats living in a network of burrows in the shallow coral sands. After 1948 Engebi was exposed repeatedly to atomic detonations, and in 1952 the whole island was swept clean of growth and overwashed by waves from the thermonuclear explosion of Operation Ivy. On each of these occasions, exposure of the rat colony to radiation was intense. In 1952, by later estimates, the animals aboveground received radiation doses of 2500 to 6000 roentgens per hour, and those in burrows doses of 112 to 1112 roentgens per hour.[19] The island environment was so altered by atomic forces and by contaminated water that radiobiologists believed it impossible that any of the rats had survived. Because there was no natural route by which the island could be repopulated, scientists even considered introducing a new rat colony for study of a population growth in a mildly radioactive environment.

---

[19] A roentgen is a unit of exposure to radiation, measuring the alteration of the atoms (ionization) of the radiated tissues. The rat dosages compare with recommended limits of exposure to man-made radiation for average individuals in human populations of an amount that approximates 0.5 roentgen per year.

Engebi Island, Eniwetok Atoll, home of a colony of rats living in radioactive surroundings.

Close-up shows one burrow in the soil.

Contrary to all expectations, however, the original colony had not been eliminated. Biologists visiting Engebi in 1953 and 1954 found the rats apparently flourishing. New generations of rats were being born and were subsisting on grasses and other plants in an environment still slightly radioactive. In 1955 analysis of the bones of rats revealed the presence of strontium-89 and strontium-90 in amounts approaching what was assumed to be the maximum amount that would not cause bodily harm. The rats' muscle tissues contained radioactive cesium-137. But no physical malformations were found in the rats. All animals appeared in sound physical condition, despite these body burdens of radioactivity. By 1964 the rat population had so increased that it apparently had reached equilibrium with available food supplies.

Questions relating to the reestablishment of the colony are intriguing. Why are new generations of these warm-blooded animals continuing to thrive after the colony was exposed to devastating nuclear effects? Is there a different dose-effect relation for these rats than for other animals? Even if it is assumed, as it must be, that some members of the colony survived the original nuclear heat and radioactivity because they were shielded by concrete bunkers or other man-made structures, how is it that there have been no observable effects among rats existing for years in an area that continually exposed them to radiation?

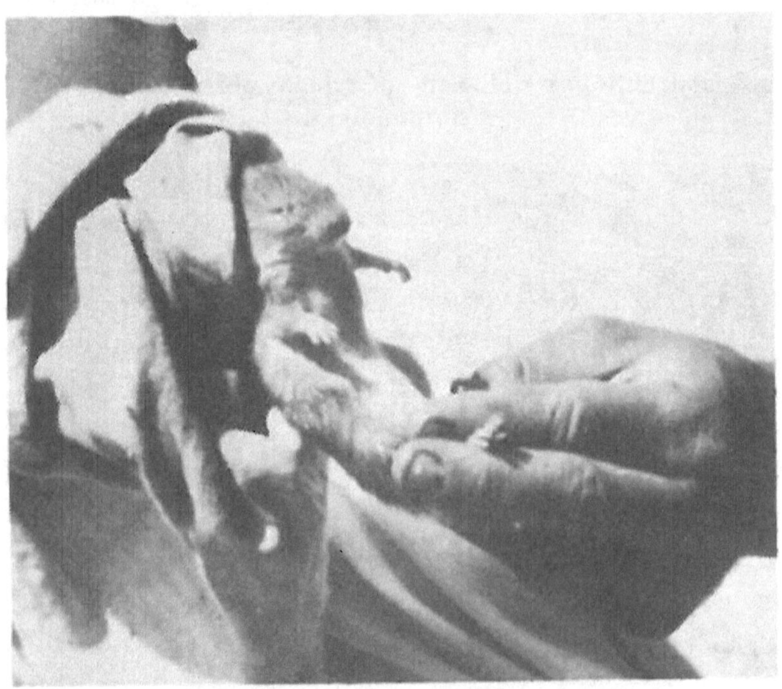

A native rat, captured alive on Engebi Island, being held by a scientist before having its toenails clipped as a means of identification. Note the animal's healthy appearance.

FALLOUT AND POPULATIONS

In Arctic regions lying on opposite sides of the North Pole, fallout has created conditions that are given continuous scrutiny by scientists of Scandinavia and the United States.

The two cases, one involving the Lapps of northern Finland and the other the Eskimos of Alaska, are essentially the same. Hemispheric fallout introduced quantities of long-lived radionuclides, particularly cesium-137, into the food chains and consequently into the diets of native peoples. In each instance there had occurred a slow accumulation of radionuclides in the lichens and mosses and in other plants that are the foods of the reindeer and caribou. The meat of these animals forms a substantial part of the human diets, and as a result the members of the native communities were found to have, on the average, body burdens of radioactivity approaching the acceptable limit for human populations.

A preliminary study of the Lapp environment was made in 1958-1959, and a Lapp dietary study was made in 1960. The results showed close correlation between the consumption of reindeer meat and the Lapps' body burdens of cesium-137. The Scandinavian investigators concluded that the levels of concentrated cesium approximated the maximum permissible dose range for large populations. They noted, however, that "the final answer ... has to be given by the geneticists".

Placing equipment to measure fallout in precipitation north of the Arctic Circle in Alaska.

In Alaska, where studies of the native populations have been proceeding for several years, adult Eskimos living in the vicinity of Anaktuvuk Pass[20] were found in 1964 to have average body burdens of cesium-137 more than 20 times as great as the average for adults in the area of the original 48 states. There was an ex-

---

[20] The area where highest readings were obtained in the survey. These studies are described in more detail in *Whole Body Counters,* a companion booklet in this series.

pectation that even without further nuclear testing the levels of cesium-137 would continue to rise slowly in Arctic regions until about 1968.

THE VARIETY OF APPROACHES

Bioenvironmental studies form a background against which all atomic energy research is conducted. The central objective of the Atomic Energy Commission's environmental radiation studies is "to determine the fate and effect of radionuclides in the environment". This objective calls for hundreds of concurrent approaches to the interlocking problems of the air, the sea, and the land. The AEC alone, through its Division of Biology and Medicine, is supporting research costing about $75 million a year, about two-thirds of this amount going to biological and medical programs at AEC laboratories and the remainder to some 650 individual contract studies at universities, nonprofit institutions, and commercial research organizations. Additional programs, large and small, are supported by foundations or other agencies. Work goes on in other nations. Many programs are international. Although only a fraction of this total activity is specifically related to environmental problems, the concern throughout is with the effect, for good or ill, of radioactivity on man and his world. It is possible to suggest by example the lines of inquiry.

A University of Georgia Research Institute ecologist studying biological specimens in a controlled environment near the AEC Savannah River Plant, Aiken, South Carolina.

The Trinity site in New Mexico, scene of the first atomic detonation in history, was studied for a number of years after 1945, particularly in relation to the distribution and effects of residual radioactivity in the desert environment. In 1963 and 1964 scientists from the University of Missouri undertook to determine the state of revegetation of the original atomic bomb crater.

The Nevada Test Site, where nuclear programs have been conducted for a decade and a half, has invited investigations of revegetation. Project Sedan, an underground thermonuclear detonation in 1962, established conditions for one such study. The crater produced by this detonation was 320 feet deep and 1200 feet in diameter. Vegetation growing within 2500 feet of ground zero was almost completely destroyed, and the original soil was covered by radioactive throwout. Shrubs as far as 5000 feet away from ground zero were damaged by air blast, and, in the weeks after the detonation, plants within a two-mile radius were covered by radioactive sand and silt or by deposits of windblown radioactive dust.

Studies in 1963 by scientists from the University of California at Los Angeles showed that native plants—Russian thistle and various annuals—had become well established in the zone around the Sedan crater where the earth was thrown out. This area had remained barren for less than a year. Some of the shrubs most severely damaged by the blast, and exposed to cumulative gamma radiation doses of more than 4000 roentgens, had produced new growth. Populations of creosote bush, evergreen plants that in 1962 appeared to have been killed by heavy doses of radiation, were producing leafy branches in the summer of 1963. These developments permitted no conclusions, of course, for the possible radiation effects still needed to be identified. Studies were conducted, for example, of the effect of deliberately depositing nonradioactive dust on healthy creosote plants, and comparative studies of other phenomena were made.

Since 1959, ecological studies have been carried forward at the Nevada site by investigators from Brigham Young University who are interested in the abundance, seasonal occurrence, and ecological influences affecting the vertebrate and invertebrate animals in plant communities of the region. Surveys have been made in areas where nuclear explosions had obliterated natural ecological relationships and in similar areas undisturbed by nuclear effects. The investigations are concerned primarily with desert ecology—with the identification of biotic communities and of predominant animal species.

Among research programs in marine environments is that initiated in 1963 and 1964 by the University of California's Institute of Marine Resources at La Jolla, where studies of marine food chains are conducted by a team of zoologists, chemists, botanists, and microbiologists. The program studies the interrelations among organisms at the lower levels of the food chains and the dynamics of marine phytoplankton cell division, photosynthesis, and excretion of organic matter as related to temperature, light intensity, and nutrient conditions. The work is conceived as a basic study of marine ecology. It is focused, however, on questions found to be significant in studies of radioactivity in the sea.

The University of California's Lawrence Radiation Laboratory has launched a long-term investigation of the effects of the release of radionuclides on the biosphere, which encompasses the origins, transport, and final localization of radionuclides in all types of organs, tissues, cells, and subcellular constituents. The objective is "to develop the most complete understanding possible of the potential hazards to man that arise from the release of nuclear radiation and radionuclides into the biosphere and to apply this knowledge to the prevention of damage to living forms...".

In programs such as these—multiplied by hundreds—the problems are being attacked.

WHERE ARE WE NOW?

Radiobiological studies that are environmental in scope became, with the release of atomic energy, a mandate on the twentieth century.

Environmental studies are not new. They have been implicit in thousands of biological research efforts, large and small, for generations. Atomic energy, however, is a new factor. Also new is the intensity of the approach. Not until the explosion of inquiry of this century has man brought together the necessary resources—the time, the funds, the instruments, the ingenious technological devices, the ideas, and the organizational and management skills—to attack problems that are global in scale.

The atom as a tool of the environmental radiobiologist has, of itself, solved few problems. Its significance is that it has speeded up—to a degree still not fully tested—our ability to study ecosystems and their relations to each other.

The first two decades of the Atomic Age have comprised a period of swift maturity. Much has been done to gain perspective. Atomic energy as a potential force for destruction has not been controlled. But there is a surer knowledge of the hazard inherent in the absence of control and a rational hope that the new power will be directed toward peaceful objectives. We know that:

1. The uninhibited release of nuclear products into the environment of the earth will create problems—fundamentally biological problems—of long duration and of still-unassessed ultimate effect.

2. Use of atomic weapons in war could have a "biological cost" beyond calculation.

Yet, in terms of constructive employment of atomic resources, we also know that:

1. Atomic energy may help solve the very problems that the new age presents.

2. Careful and controlled development of atomic forces will provide the reservoirs of energy that will be needed to sustain the world's populations of the next century and beyond.

In whatever case, the solutions lie in the direction of environmental knowledge.

Man, the human animal, will live in the environment he has the intelligence to understand and to preserve.

THE FIRST TWENTY YEARS

Instruments for environmental research. A radiation analyzer for laboratory examination of field samples.

Installing environmental research equipment in the field.

"... All creatures are linked to each other ... in their dependence on limited environments that together form the whole of nature ..." (Page 3). (White-capped noddy tern nesting colony, Engebi Island, Eniwetok Atoll, photographed in 1965.)

SUGGESTED REFERENCES

BASIC

Sourcebook on Atomic Energy, Samuel Glasstone, D. Van Nostrand Company, Inc., Princeton, New Jersey, 1958, 641 pp., $4.40.

What is Ionizing Radiation?, Robert L. Platzman, *Scientific American*, 201: 74 (September 1959).

WEAPONS TESTING AND FALLOUT

The Effects of Nuclear Weapons, Samuel Glasstone (Ed.), U. S. Atomic Energy Commission, 1962 (revised edition), 730 pp., $3.00. Available from Superintendent of Documents, U. S. Government Printing Office, Washington, D. C. 20402.

Fallout from Nuclear Weapons Tests, Hearings Before the Special Subcommittee on Radiation of the Joint Committee on Atomic Energy, 86th Congress, First Session, Superintendent of Documents, U. S. Government Printing Office, Washington, D. C. 20402, 1959. Vol. I, 948 pp., $2.75; Vol. II, 1967 pp., $2.75; Vol. III, 2618 pp., $1.75. "Summary-Analysis of Hearings", 42 pp., $0.15, is available only from the Office of the Joint Committee on Atomic Energy, Congress of the United States, Washington, D. C. 20510.

Bombs at Bikini, W. A. Shurcliff, William H. Wise & Co., Inc., New York, 1947, 212 pp., $3.50. Out of print but available through libraries.

BIOLOGICAL EFFECTS OF RADIATION

Health Implications of Fallout from Nuclear Weapons Testing Through 1961 (Report No. 3), Federal Radiation Council, Washington, D. C., May 1962, 10 pp., free.

Estimates and Evaluation of Fallout in the United States from Nuclear Weapons Testing Conducted Through 1962 (Report No. 4), Federal Radiation Council, Washington, D. C., May 1963, 41 pp., $0.30.

Report of the United Nations Scientific Committee on the Effects of Atomic Radiation, General Assembly, Seventeenth Session, Supplement No. 16 (A/5216), United Nations, International Documents Service, Columbia University Press, New York, 1962, 146 pp., $5.00.

RADIOACTIVITY IN THE ENVIRONMENT

Environmental Radioactivity, Merril Eisenbud, McGraw-Hill Book Company, Inc., New York, 1963, 430 pp., $12.50.

Proving Ground: An Account of the Radiobiological Studies in the Pacific, 1946-1961, Neal O. Hines, University of Washington Press, Seattle, Washington, 1962, 366 pp., $6.75.

Radioecology, Proceedings of the First National Symposium on Radioecology Held at Colorado State University, Fort Collins, Colorado, September 10-15, 1961, Vincent Schultz and Alfred W. Klement, Jr. (Eds.), published jointly by the Reinhold Publishing Corporation, New York, and the American Institute of Biological Sciences, Washington, D. C., 746 pp., $16.50. Available from Reinhold.

The Circulation of Radioisotopes, J. A. Arnold and E. A. Martell, *Scientific American*, 201: 84 (September 1959).

The following reports are available from the Clearinghouse for Federal Scientific and Technical Information, 5285 Port Royal Road, Springfield, Virginia 22151.

Radioactive Fallout from Nuclear Weapons Tests (TID-7632), Proceedings of a Conference held in Germantown, Maryland, November 15–17, 1961, Alfred W. Klement, Jr. (Ed.), U. S. Atomic Energy Commission, Division of Technical Information, 546 pp., $5.75.

Radio active Fallout from Nuclear Weapons Tests (CONF-765), Proceedings of a Conference held in Germantown, Maryland, November 3–6, 1964, Alfred W. Klement, Jr. (Ed.), U. S. Atomic Energy Commission, Division of Technical Information, 953 pp., $6.50.

Bioenvironmental Features of the Ogotoruk Area, Cape Thompson, Alaska (TID-17226), A Second Summary by the Committee on Environmental Studies for Project Chariot, Bette Weichold (Ed.), U. S. Atomic Energy Commission, Division of Technical Information, 183 pp., January 1965, $2.75.

MOTION PICTURES

Available for loan without charge from the AEC Headquarters Film Library, Division of Pubic Information, U.S. Atomic Energy Commission, Washington, D.C. 20545, and from other AEC film libraries.

Bikini Radiological Laboratory, 22 minutes, sound, colour, 1949. Produced by the University of Washington and the U.S. Atomic Energy Commission. This nontechnical film, for intermedia-through college-level audiences, explains studies of effects of radioactivity from the 1946 atomic test at Bikini Atoll on plants and marine life in the area 3 years later.

Return to Bikini, 50 minutes, sound, colour, 1964. Produced by the Laboratory of Radiation Biology at the University of Washington for the U.S. Atomic Energy Commission. This film records the ecological resurvey of Bikini in 1964, six years after the last weapons test.

PHOTO CREDITS

35	F Brigham Young University
37	PRNC
39	Hanford Plant
40	ORNL
41	LRB
42	PNL
43	PNL
46	A PRNC
46	B LRB
47	C LRB
47	D PNL
48	E PNL
48	F U.S. Bureau of Commercial Fisheries
50-51	ORNL
53	LRB
54	BGSU
55	PNL
56	UG
60	UG (left)
60	PNL (right)
61	BGSU

Key:

BGSU	Bowling Green state University
BNL	Brookhaven National Laboratory
LRB	Laboratory of Radiation Biology, University of Washington
ORNL	Oak Ridge National Laboratory
PNL	Pacific Northwest Laboratory
PRNC	Puerto Rico Nuclear Center
UG	University of Georgia
MAPS	on pages 8, 12, and 24 from Proving Ground, Neal O. Hines

Lector House believes that a society develops through a two-fold approach of continuous learning and adaptation, which is derived from the study of classic literary works spread across the historic timeline of literature records. Therefore, we aim at reviving, repairing and redeveloping all those inaccessible or damaged but historically as well as culturally important literature across subjects so that the future generations may have an opportunity to study and learn from past works to embark upon a journey of creating a better future.

This book is a result of an effort made by Lector House towards making a contribution to the preservation and repair of original ancient works which might hold historical significance to the approach of continuous learning across subjects.

HAPPY READING & LEARNING!

LECTOR HOUSE LLP
E-MAIL: lectorpublishing@gmail.com

www.ingramcontent.com/pod-product-compliance
Lightning Source LLC
LaVergne TN
LVHW091526170726
843492LV00004B/1087